Mommy's

Weaning from Breastfeeding Together

Sarit Guy IBCLC

At first,
all I wanted was to **nurse**.

Nurse on the bed or on the chair,
nurse and nurse without a care.

Mommy nursed me with every sneeze,
with every yawn, or every squeeze
whenever I pleased.

If I cried or had a scare
- mommy's milk was always there.

I didn't drink or eat any food,
I just nursed and it was good.
I slept all day,
I couldn't even play.

But slowly I grew,

and found things that were new!

I started to laugh and smile,

grab a toy for a short while,

roll around – crawled almost a mile!

I was a baby, so small,

but now a **big boy!**

I want to know it all!

I try new things to eat,

new flavors – sour, salty and sweet!

Eating is fun!

I try and like almost everything, yum!

With a spoon, a fork,
or just my hands.
Eat by myself? Yes, **I can!**

From time to time, I still nurse, and do a little trick,

I nurse and stand on one leg. Look, mommy, quick!

Sometimes, I tickle my mommy, or tease,

or move from one side to the other

with ease.

But sometimes, I'm too busy to stop,

to take a break and nurse, not even a drop.

I'm a very **busy boy**!

There are many things I enjoy.

I like to walk, dance and hop,

climb up the slide, right to the top.

And other things I enjoy?

Hearing stories and playing with toys!

I feel so **big**, as tall as the sky,

so I can say to mommy's booby – bye-bye.

Thank you, mommy, for your caresses and hugs,
you nursed me and made sure I was snug.

Thanks for your warm milk and loving heart,
your milk helped me grow and get very smart!

Now that we said booby **bye-bye**, it's done,

let's goof around and have lots of **fun!**

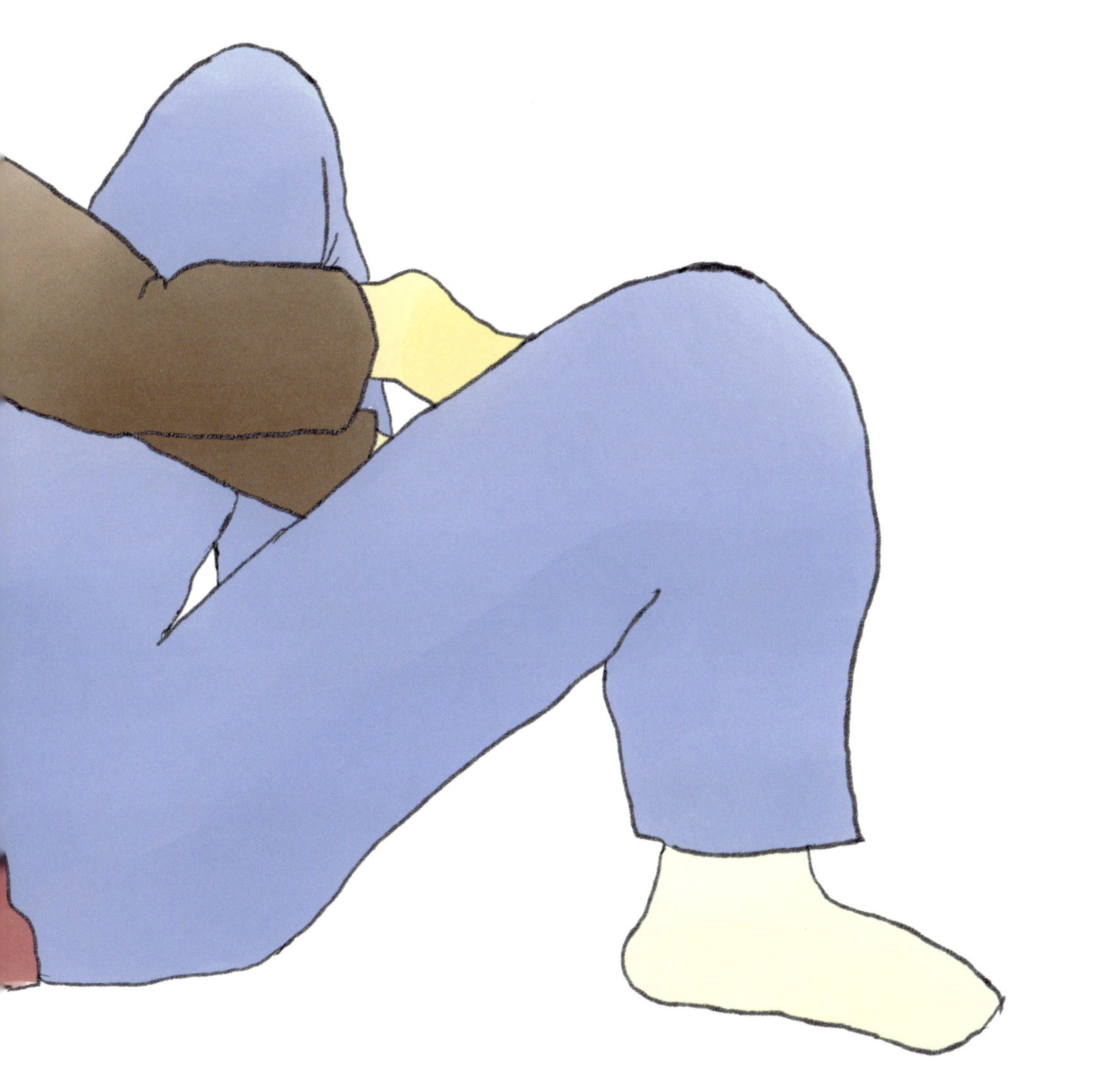

And what will happen when I'll be grumpy or mad,
when I'll need my mommy close because I'm sad?
What if I wake from a scary dream,
and miss the booby so much that I scream?

Mommy has a **special hug**, just for me.
It's only mine as cuddly as can be.

If I get a little tired or sad,
or want to feel snug

I don't need mommy's booby,
instead, **I have her hug!**

How to use the book:

This book serves as a tool throughout the weaning process.
You can start reading the book even before starting to wean, as preparation for the weaning process and during the process itself. It is recommended to read the story, look at the pictures together and encourage a conversation with your child.
The messages in this story contribute to the process of weaning from breastfeeding, making it a positive and empowering experience for both you and your child.
I recommend incorporating these messages when talking to your child.

Message #1: Weaning from breastfeeding is a positive stage in a child's maturing process.
Just as we are proud of our children for every new developmental stage, such as potty training, so we should be proud when they are ready to wean from breastfeeding.

Message #2: Creating a positive memory of the breastfeeding period.
We had an amazing time together and now it is time to say goodbye to breastfeeding in a positive way. It is important to note how pleasant and good breastfeeding was for both the mother and child. By doing so, we create a positive experience and a sweet memory for the child, remembering the shared magical period of breastfeeding.

Message #3: Mommy is always here with you even without breastfeeding.
This is an important message that should be passed on to the child during the weaning process. It is a message that instills a sense of confidence. Mommy is still here to hug, soothe, empathize, comfort and support, even after the child has been weaned from breastfeeding.

During the weaning process, I also recommend to always concentrate on the positive and to tell the child what we "have" and not only what we "do not have." So, while there is no more breastfeeding, the physical embrace and emotional connection always remain.

Even after the breastfeeding period is over, this book can be used as a special keepsake. The child can still flip through it and remember that beautiful time together.

I wish you an empowering and bonding weaning process.
Good luck!
Sarit Guy, Certified Lactation Consultant – IBCLC

Mommy's Hug

Weaning from breastfeeding together

Sarit Guy IBCLC

Self-published by Sarit Guy
Graphics design: Neomie Yulzary
Translated by: Dr. English
Counselor to the English version: Blair Allon – Lactation consultant

Milk & Honey +972-585455261 www.halavd.co.il

My family

(Illustration: Meirav Guy, 11 years old)

Made in the USA
Columbia, SC
25 April 2025